UNITED ARAB EMIRATES

The United Arab Emirates (UAE) is a federation of seven semiautonomous emirates with a resident population of approximately six million, of whom approximately 20 percent (one million) are citizens. The rulers of the seven emirates constitute the Federal Supreme Council, the country's highest legislative and executive body. The council selects a president and a vice president from its membership, and the president appoints the prime minister and cabinet. In 2004 the council selected Sheikh Khalifa bin Zayed al-Nahyan, ruler of Abu Dhabi Emirate, as head of state for a five-year term. In November 2009 the council reselected Sheikh Khalifa to a second term as president. The emirates are under patriarchal rule with political allegiance defined by loyalty to tribal leaders, to leaders of the individual emirates, and to leaders of the federation. There are no democratically elected legislative institutions or political parties. There are no general elections. Citizens can express their concerns directly to their leaders through traditional, consultative mechanisms such as the open "majlis" (forum). The Federal National Council (FNC), a consultative body, consists of 40 representatives, 20 elected by an appointed electorate in 2006. Security forces reported to civilian authorities.

Citizens did not have the right to change their government. There were unverified reports of torture during the year, and security forces sometimes employed flogging as judicially sanctioned punishment. Arbitrary and incommunicado detention remained a problem. The judiciary lacked independence. The government interfered with privacy and restricted civil liberties, including freedoms of speech, press (including the Internet), assembly, association, and religion. There were limited reports of corruption, and the government lacked transparency. Domestic abuse of women remained a problem, and there were allegations that police sometimes enabled domestic abuse. Legal and societal discrimination against women and noncitizens was pervasive. Trafficking in persons continued, the government severely restricted the rights of foreign workers, and abuse of foreign domestic servants remained problematic.

RESPECT FOR HUMAN RIGHTS

Section 1   Respect for the Integrity of the Person, Including Freedom From:

    a.   Arbitrary or Unlawful Deprivation of Life

There were no reports that the government or its agents committed arbitrary or unlawful killings.

b. Disappearance

There were no reports of politically motivated disappearances.

c. Torture and Other Cruel, Inhuman, or Degrading Treatment or Punishment

The constitution prohibits such practices; however, there were reports that government officials employed them, especially towards foreigners in detention. In January a court acquitted a member of the ruling family of Abu Dhabi, implicated by videotape for the 2004 torture of a foreign national, allegedly over a business dispute. Human rights groups decried the acquittal as a sign of the lack of judicial independence.

Sharia (Islamic law) courts occasionally imposed flogging as punishment for adultery, prostitution, consensual premarital sex, pregnancy outside marriage, defamation of character, and drug or alcohol abuse. Authorities used canes to administer floggings, resulting in substantial bruising, welts, and open wounds on those flogged.

There were also reports of prison guard brutality during the year. On September 1, local media reported that 17 Indian nationals convicted of murder in March claimed in their appeal hearing that their confessions were obtained after a severe beating from police in Dubai. Their convictions were overturned on appeal in December.

Prison and Detention Center Conditions

Prison conditions varied widely between emirates. Some prisons were overcrowded, particularly in Abu Dhabi and Dubai. Conditions for female prisoners were equal to or slightly better than those for men. Prisoners convicted on national security grounds were held separately from the general population in special state security facilities. Conditions in these special sections were not different from other parts of the prisons. Prisoners had access to visitors, but it was unclear if they were permitted religious observance. Prisoners have a right to submit complaints to judicial authorities; however, details about investigations into complaints were not publicly available.

There were credible reports that government officials discriminated against prisoners with HIV by separating them from the general prison population and by not granting commuted sentences or parole that other prisoners with similar records received. Others did not have access to appropriate health care in detention.

On September 2, local media reported the suicide of an Emirati prisoner in a Dubai jail. The prisoner reportedly was mentally ill and held in solitary confinement, where he committed suicide.

Police in Dubai and Abu Dhabi stated that nongovernmental organizations (NGOs) and the International Committee of the Red Cross had access to observe prison conditions if requested. The government stated that it inspected and monitored prison and detention center conditions. However, in 2008 when members of the NGO Emirates Human Rights Association (EHRA) visited female inmates at Dubai's al-Aweer Detention Facility, prison authorities denied the monitors access "to protect the prisoners' social and psychological rights." Charitable NGOs visited prisons during the year and were permitted to provide material support. They were unable to determine the welfare of the prisoners.

Ombudsmen cannot serve on behalf of prisoners and detainees.

d.   Arbitrary Arrest or Detention

The constitution prohibits arbitrary arrest and detention; however, there were reports that the government held persons in official custody without charge or a preliminary judicial hearing. The Ministry of Interior detained foreign residents arbitrarily at times. The law permits indefinite, routine, incommunicado detention without appeal. Under this procedure, the detainee may contact only an attorney but is not permitted to see friends and family.

Role of the Police and Security Apparatus

The federal Ministry of Interior (Ministry of Interior) oversees police general directorates in all of the seven emirates; each emirate, under its corresponding police general directorate, maintains its own police force and supervises police stations. All emirate police forces are officially branches of the ministry; in practice they operated with considerable autonomy. The police forces are responsible for internal security, and the federal armed forces are responsible for external security.

Local police are semiautonomous, and the Ministry of Interior has broad authority to investigate abuses.

On August 25, courts in Dubai convicted two Emirati police officers of kidnapping, unlawful arrest, abuse of authority, and theft. The officers reportedly detained street vendors, locked them in police vehicles, and stole the vendors' money.

On August 26, a Dubai court heard testimony from a British woman who alleged an Emirati soldier raped her. The victim claimed she was beaten and raped twice, once in the soldier's car and once in her Dubai apartment. The case continued at year's end.

No information was available on the outcome of the 2009 case of a Sharjah police officer charged with kidnap and rape in Dubai.

Civilian authorities maintained effective control over the local police forces, and the government had effective mechanisms to investigate and punish abuse and corruption. There were no reports of impunity involving security forces during the year.

Arrest Procedures and Treatment While in Detention

The law prohibits arrest or search of citizens without probable cause; however, incidents occurred in practice. There were reports that security forces failed to obtain warrants in some cases.

Police stations received complaints from the public, made arrests, and forwarded cases to the public prosecutor. The public prosecutor then transferred cases to the courts. In cases involving foreign defendants, especially for crimes of moral turpitude, authorities often summarily deported the defendants upon completion of their jail terms. Police must report an arrest within 48 hours to the public prosecutor, who then must determine within 24 hours whether to charge, release, or further detain the suspect. In practice the public prosecutor did not always meet the 24-hour time limit, although police usually adhered to their 48-hour deadline. Public prosecutors may order detainees held as long as 21 days without charge or longer, in some cases, with a court order. Courts may not grant an extension of more than 30 days of detention without charge; however, judges may renew 30-day extensions indefinitely. Public prosecutors may hold suspects in terrorism-related cases without charge for six months. Once a suspect is charged, the Supreme Court handles terrorism cases, which may extend the detention period indefinitely.

There is no formal system of bail; however, authorities temporarily can release detainees who deposit money, a passport, or an unsecured personal guarantee statement signed by a third party. Defendants in cases involving loss of life, including involuntary manslaughter, may be denied release in accordance with the law. Some prisoners, detained on charges related to a person's death, were released after making a monetary payment to the victim's family, called a "diya" (or "blood money").

A defendant is entitled to an attorney after police have completed their investigation. Police sometimes questioned the accused for weeks without access to an attorney. Generally authorities granted family members prompt access to those arrested on charges unrelated to state security. The government may provide counsel, at its discretion, to indigent defendants charged with felonies that are punishable by imprisonment of three to 15 years.

Amnesty

On religious and national holidays, rulers of each emirate regularly pardon, and pay the debts of many prisoners. According to press reports, rulers pardoned at least 2,090 prisoners and paid their debts during the year. In October the new ruler of Ras Al Khaimah pardoned 140 individuals in honor of his late father. The government deported most of the pardoned foreign nationals.

e.   Denial of Fair Public Trial

The constitution provides for an independent judiciary; however, in practice court decisions remained subject to review by the political leadership and suffered greatly from nepotism. There were reports that the federal intelligence service, the Directorate of State Security, intervened in judicial affairs. The judiciary was composed largely of contracted foreign nationals subject to potential deportation. There was no functional separation between the executive and judicial branches.

By tradition the local rulers' offices, or "diwans," maintained the practice of reviewing some criminal and civil offenses before they referred cases to prosecutors. They also reviewed sentences judges passed, returned cases to the court on appeal if they did not approve of the verdict, and approved the release of every prisoner who had completed a sentence. The diwans' involvement--usually in cases between two citizens or between a citizen and noncitizen--led to lengthy delays prior to and following the judicial process and lengthened the time defendants served in prison. The diwan's decision in any court case is considered final and, when a judge and diwan disagree, the diwan's decision prevails.

There is a dual court system. Sharia courts adjudicate criminal and family law matters based on each emirate's interpretation of Sharia. Civil courts adjudicate civil law matters and, except in the emirates of Dubai, Abu Dhabi, and Ras al-Khaimah, are accountable to the Federal Supreme Court, which has the power of judicial review, as well as original jurisdiction in disputes between emirates or between the federal government and individual emirates. Dubai, Abu Dhabi, and Ras al-Khaimah emirates are not subject to routine review by the Federal Supreme court, although they can refer individual cases to the court.

The military has its own court system and military tribunals try only military personnel. Only the Federal Supreme Court hears national security cases.

Trial Procedures

According to the law, defendants are presumed innocent until proven guilty. The constitution provides the right to a public trial, except in national security cases or cases the judge deems harmful to public morality. There are no jury trials. Defendants have the right to be present at their trial and a limited right to legal counsel in court. While awaiting a decision on official charges at the police station or the prosecutor's office, a defendant is not entitled to legal counsel. In all cases involving a capital crime or possible life imprisonment, the defendant has a right to government-provided counsel. The government may also provide counsel, at its discretion, to indigent defendants charged with felonies punishable by imprisonment of three to 15 years. The law provides prosecutors discretion to bar defense counsel from any investigation. Defendants and their attorneys can present witnesses and question witnesses against them. Defense counsel has access to relevant government-held evidence. By law all court proceedings are conducted in Arabic. Despite the defendant's procedural right to a translator, in some cases involving deportation of illegal residents, the court provided translation only at sentencing. The defense counsel often used a translator to communicate with the defendant.

Each court system has an appeals process. Death sentences may be appealed to the ruler of the emirate in which the offense is committed or to the president of the federation. In murder cases, only the victim's family may commute a death sentence. The government normally negotiates with victims' families for the defendant to offer diya in exchange for forgiveness and a commuted death sentence.

In cases that end in acquittals, the prosecutor may appeal and provide new or additional evidence to a higher court. An appellate court must reach unanimous agreement to overturn an acquittal.

In the ongoing case of an American citizen charged with financial crimes, the Courts and Prosecutor's office demonstrated preferential treatment to the Emirati codefendant. The court also used procedures that extended his incarceration. Police and prosecutor appeared to work to circumvent court orders that offered bail by holding cases in "investigative" status and raising additional cases against the defendant that require new rulings from the judge. These practices kept the accused incarcerated throughout the year, while other non-foreign and Emirati defendants in similar cases were allowed to defend their cases outside incarceration, in bail status.

Political Prisoners and Detainees

There were no reports of political prisoners or detainees; however, there were persons reportedly held incommunicado and without charge for unknown reasons.

Civil Judicial Procedures and Remedies

Citizens and noncitizens had access to the courts to seek damages for, or cessation of, human rights violations. The civil courts, like all courts in the country, lacked independence. Administrative remedies were available for labor complaints and were particularly common in cases regarding physical abuse of domestic workers.

f.   Arbitrary Interference with Privacy, Family, Home, or Correspondence

The constitution prohibits entry into a home without the owner's permission, except when police present a warrant in accordance with the law, but there were credible reports that security forces occasionally failed to obtain warrants. Officers' actions in searching premises were subject to review by the Ministry of Interior, and officers were liable to disciplinary action if their actions were judged irresponsible. Unlike in the previous year, there were no reports of censorship of incoming international mail.

The constitution provides for freedom and confidentiality of correspondence by mail, telegram, and all other means of communication. However, in July 2009 the primary telecommunications provider offered a BlackBerry user update that included surveillance and interception software. Citing a technical problem, later that month the firm provided customers instructions on how to remove the program. All electronic communication remained secure and private during the year.

Local interpretation of Sharia prohibits Muslim women from marrying non-Muslims and Muslim men from marrying women not "of the book," meaning adherents of religions other than Islam, Christianity, and Judaism.

Section 2   Respect for Civil Liberties, Including:

a.   Freedom of Speech and Press

The constitution provides for freedom of speech and of the press; however, the government restricted these rights in practice. The law prohibits criticism of rulers and speech that may create or encourage social unrest. Journalists and editors practiced extensive self-censorship for fear of government retribution, particularly since most journalists were foreign nationals and could be deported.

Public criticism of the government and ministers was permissible in a limited context, but criticism of ruling families, particularly sheikhs, was not permitted. Some books perceived as critical of the government were not available for sale.

In January authorities dismissed a government employee and advisor to the Ras al Khaimah crown prince after the employee criticized the lack of press freedom in the country in a television interview. The employee's passport was withheld, and no information on its return was available at year's end.

The government owned three of the country's newspapers and heavily influenced the privately owned media, particularly through government subsidies. A free trade zone in Dubai dedicated to media-related business is administered separately and operates under separate bylaws. Except for media located in this free zone and foreign language media targeted to foreign residents, most television and radio stations were government-owned and conformed to unpublished government reporting guidelines. Foreign journalists and news organizations operating from the Dubai Media Free Zone reported no restrictions on the content of print and broadcast material produced for use outside the country. Satellite-receiving dishes were widespread and provided access to international broadcasts without apparent censorship.

By law the National Media Council (NMC), appointed by the president, licenses and censors all publications, including private association publications. Media outlets must inform the NMC of the appointment of editors, and the NMC is responsible for issuing press credentials. The law authorizes censorship of domestic and foreign publications to remove criticism of the government, ruling families, or friendly governments, as well as other statements that "threaten social stability." According to the council and Dubai police officials, journalists were not given specific publishing instructions; however, government officials reportedly warned journalists when they published material deemed politically or culturally sensitive. Journalists practiced extensive self-censorship regarding the issues they chose to cover.

The government used libel laws to suppress criticism of its leaders. No journalists have received prison sentences for defamation since 2007. Other punishments for violations of libel laws remained in force, including suspension of publishing for a specified period of time and penalties of five million dirhams (approximately $1.4 million) for disparaging senior officials or royal family members and 500,000 dirhams (approximately $140,000) for misleading the public and harming the country's reputation, foreign relations, or economy. On September 28, the international NGO the Committee to Protect Journalists issued a statement to the press calling for the fair treatment of a Dubai-based reporter, Mark Townsend, charged with defamation in August for allegedly criticizing his employer, *Khaleej Times*, in a series of online posts. Information on the trial was not available at year's end.

The NMC censors reviewed all imported media and prohibited or censored before distribution any material considered pornographic, excessively violent, derogatory to Islam, supportive of certain Israeli government positions, unduly critical of friendly countries, or critical of the government or ruling families. The authorities treated the publication of books in the same manner.

Internet Freedom

The government restricted access to some Web sites and monitored chat rooms, instant messaging services, and blogs. There were few reports of government prosecution or punishment, although self-censorship was apparent in many chat rooms and blogs. The *UN Human Development Report* estimated there were more than 300 Internet users per 1,000 persons in 2009. Local media reported that the Ministry of Interior monitored Internet use in cybercafés.

The country's only two service providers, used a proxy server to block material deemed inconsistent with the country's values, as defined by the Ministry of Interior. Blocked material included dating and matrimonial sites; gay and lesbian sites; sites concerning the Bahai faith; some sites originating in Israel; and sites explaining how to circumvent the proxy server. The proxy servers occasionally blocked broad categories of sites. Service providers populated their list of blocked sites primarily from lists purchased from private companies, although individuals also could report offensive sites. A social Web site and the politically oriented Web sites remained blocked during the year. Some sites that contained content critical of ruling families were blocked. The NMC was responsible for creating lists of blocked sites. Service providers do not have the authority to remove Web sites from block lists without government approval.

The law explicitly criminalizes the use of the Internet to commit a wide variety of offenses and provides fines and prison terms for Internet users who violate political, social, and religious norms. The law also criminalizes acts commonly associated with "cyber crimes," such as hacking, "phishing," and other forms of financial fraud. The law provides penalties for using the Internet to oppose Islam, proselytize Muslims to join other religions, "abuse" a holy shrine or ritual of any religion, insult any religion, incite someone to commit sin, or transcend "family values" by publishing news or photos pertaining to a person's private life or family.

Academic Freedom and Cultural Events

The government restricted academic freedom and censored academic materials for schools. The government prohibited students from reading texts featuring sexuality or pictures of the human body including in health and biology classes. The government also restricted participation in certain cultural events, primarily events it deemed un-Islamic.

Official permission was required for conferences that discussed political issues. In May the minister of social affairs ordered the cancellation of a meeting in Dubai of the Gulf Cooperation Council Association of Sociologists relating to social security, objecting to the topic of "terrorism" being addressed in conference white papers. The minister stated that the conference organizers had failed to obtain security clearance.

b.   Freedom of Peaceful Assembly and Association

The constitution provides for freedoms of assembly and association; however, in practice the government did not respect these rights.

Freedom of Assembly

The law requires a government-issued permit for organized public gatherings. In practice the government did not interfere regularly with informal nonpolitical gatherings held without a government permit in public places unless there were complaints.

In contrast to 2009, when there were at least two reports of unauthorized public gatherings dispersed by the police, none were reported during the year; however, in July there were credible reports that authorities arrested two citizens after they attempted to organize a protest over fuel price increases. The government reportedly fired one of the organizers who worked for the Dubai police department in an administrative capacity.

Freedom of Association

Political organizations, political parties, and trade unions are illegal. All associations and NGOs were required to register with the Ministry of Social Affairs, and many received government subsidies. Approximately 100 domestic NGOs were registered with the ministry, mostly citizens' associations for economic, religious, social, cultural, athletic, and other purposes. More than 20 unregistered local NGOs that focused on nonpolitical topics operated with little to no government interference. Associations must follow the government's censorship guidelines and receive prior government approval before publishing any material.

c.   Freedom of Religion

For a complete description of religious freedom, please see the *2010 International Religious Freedom Report* at www.state.gov/g/drl/irf/rpt.

d. Freedom of Movement, Internally Displaced Persons, Protection of Refugees, and Stateless Persons

The law provides for freedom of movement within the country, emigration, and repatriation, and the government generally respected these rights in practice; however, the government imposed legal restrictions on foreign travel. The government cooperated with the Office of the UN High Commissioner for Refugees (UNHCR) and other humanitarian organizations on a humanitarian basis, but it did not grant refugee status or asylum.

Male citizens involved in legal disputes under adjudication were not permitted to travel overseas. Custom dictates that a husband can prevent his wife, minor children, and adult unmarried daughters from leaving the country by taking custody of their passports. The government may revoke naturalized citizens' passports and citizenship status for criminal or politically provocative actions. Such revocations are rare, and there were no such reports during the year.

The constitution prohibits forced exile, and there were no reported cases during the year.

Protection of Refugees

The country's laws do not provide for the granting of asylum or refugees. The country is not a party to the 1951 Convention relating to the Status of Refugees or the 1967 Protocol relating to the Status of Refugees. There is no system for providing protection to refugees, and the government did not provide protection against the expulsion or return of refugees to countries where their lives or freedom would be threatened on account of their race, religion, nationality, membership in a particular social group, or political opinion.

The government continued to detain some persons seeking refugee status, particularly Palestinians and non-Arabs, while they awaited resettlement in third countries. As access to employment, education, and other public services is based on an individual's status as a legal resident, a refugee is not eligible for such benefits.

Stateless Persons

Estimates suggested that an unverified range of 20,000 to 100,000 persons without any citizenship or proof of citizenship (known as "Bidoon") resided in the country.

Although the government improved the naturalization process in 2009, granting citizenship to 70 persons that year compared to 51 persons in 2008, no stateless person received citizenship during the year.

The government registered Bidoon births but did not grant citizenship to the children. Most Bidoon lacked citizenship because they did not have the preferred tribal affiliation used to determine citizenship when the country was established. Others had entered the country, legally or illegally, in search of employment. The Bidoon faced discrimination in employment and had restricted access to medical care and education. Without passports or other identity documents, their movement was restricted, both within the country and internationally. Local charities, some funded with government money, provided limited medical and educational services to Bidoon.

Citizenship is derived generally from one's parents. Children of female citizens married to noncitizens do not acquire citizenship automatically at birth, but their mothers can obtain citizenship for the children after submitting an application, which the government generally accepts. A foreign woman may receive citizenship through marriage to a citizen after 10 years of marriage, and anyone may receive a passport by presidential fiat.

Section 3   Respect for Political Rights: The Right of Citizens to Change Their Government

The law does not provide citizens the right to change their government peacefully. There were no democratic general elections or institutions, and citizens did not have the right to form political parties.

Federal executive and legislative power is in the hands of the Federal Supreme Council, a body composed of the hereditary rulers of the seven emirates. It elects from its members the country's president and vice president. Decisions at the federal level generally represented consensus among the rulers, their families, and other leading families. The ruling families, in consultation with other prominent tribal figures, also choose new emirate rulers.

Although the FNC has no legislative authority, it generally reviewed all federal draft laws and decrees before the Federal Supreme Council officially adopted them, and it could send legislation back for amendment. The FNC also has the authority to question any government minister, but it requires cabinet approval in order to raise a topic for discussion, and it lacks any enforcement mechanism.

Elections and Political Participation

In 2006 a 6,689-member-appointed electorate elected half of the 40-seat FNC; each emirate appoints a portion of the other 20 members. In 2008 the Federal Supreme Council announced a constitutional amendment that extended the term of FNC members from two to four years.

Some traditional practices discouraged women from engaging in political participation. However, there were four women in the cabinet; nine women, one of whom was elected, served in the FNC; and several women served as public prosecutors or judges. In Sharjah seven women served on the 40-seat Consultative Council, and two women served as directors of local departments. A few women held nonfederal senior government positions in the other emirates. Women were only 17 percent of the approximately 7,000-person electorate handpicked by the emirates' rulers to vote in FNC elections.

Except in the judiciary, minorities, including Shia, did not serve in senior federal positions. Many judges were contracted foreign nationals.

Section 4   Official Corruption and Government Transparency

The law provides criminal penalties for official corruption, and the government generally implemented the law effectively. Government corruption reportedly occurred at the administrative level. There were no financial disclosure laws for public officials.

Due to the lack of the independence of the courts, those in power or connected to the ruling families rarely were punished for corruption. Nepotism and corrupt financial and legal practices existed.

In 2008 the Department of Accountability returned to the Ministry of Finance approximately 300 million dirhams (approximately $82 million) that employees had embezzled. At year's end, there was no information regarding what had happened to the employees.

The law provides for public access to government information, but the government followed this provision selectively. Requests for access usually went unanswered.

Section 5   Governmental Attitude Regarding International and Nongovernmental Investigation of Alleged Violations of Human Rights

The government generally did not permit organizations to focus on political issues. Two recognized local human rights organizations existed: the quasi-independent EHRA, which focused on human rights issues and complaints such as labor rights, stateless persons' rights, and prisoners' well-being and humane treatment; and the government-subsidized Jurists' Association Human Rights Committee, which focused on human rights education and conducted seminars and symposia subject to government approval. Although a government prosecutor headed the EHRA, it generally operated without government interference, apart from the requirements that apply to all associations in the country. EHRA members met with Ministry of Interior officials and prisoners during visits to several detention facilities.

The government directed and subsidized participation by NGO members in events outside the country, such as for a human rights conference in Europe for members of EHRA. However, all participants must obtain government permission before attending such events, even if they are not speakers.

In 2009 the Ministry of Social Affairs rejected applications by the Jurists' Association to join the Arab Coalition for Development, Democracy, and Human Rights and the International Bar Association, and the government prevented Jurists' Association Human Rights Committee members from traveling to meetings outside the country, including meetings of the Arab Jurists Union and the Gulf Jurists Union.

The government did not allow international human rights NGOs to be based in the country but allowed representatives to visit on a limited basis. There were no transparent standards governing visits from international NGO representatives. On January 24, the international NGO Human Rights Watch held a press conference in Dubai where it released its annual report on human rights violations.

The government generally cooperated with other international organizations, including the UN Children's Fund and the UNHCR. The UN Office for the Coordination of Humanitarian Affairs maintained an office in the country, and in October the government hosted the UN special rapporteur on the sale of children, child prostitution, and child pornography.

Section 6   Discrimination, Societal Abuses, and Trafficking in Persons

The constitution provides for equality for citizens without regard to race, nationality, or social status, and the law prohibits discrimination based on disability; however, legal and cultural discrimination existed and went unpunished. The constitution does not provide for equality for noncitizens.

Women

Rape is punishable by death under the penal code, but in Sharia courts the extremely high burden of proof often meant that there were few convictions. The penal code does not address spousal rape. There were widespread and frequent reports that foreign domestic workers were raped and sexually assaulted by their employers.

Domestic abuse against women, including spousal abuse, was a common problem. The penal code allows men to use physical means, including violence, at their discretion against female and minor family members. Nevertheless, some domestic abuse cases may be filed as assault without intent to kill, punishable by 10 years in prison if death results, seven years for permanent disability, and one year for temporary injury. Such cases were rare. Victims of domestic abuse may file complaints with police units stationed in major public hospitals. There were several reports that police refused to protect women if they made such complaints; instead, police reportedly encouraged women to return home. In some cases, authorities contacted the allegedly abusive husbands to transport their wives home.

On October 5, the Federal Supreme Court upheld a husband's right to "chastise" his wife and children with physical force, so long as the "chastisement" did not result in bruising. On October 8, the director of the Judicial Inspection Department at the Ministry of Justice, Humaid al Muhairi, released a statement clarifying the government's position on domestic abuse, saying that the "full force of the law will continue to be brought against those who may exercise chastisement of any kind, verbal or otherwise, beyond acceptable bounds."

Social workers and counselors, usually female, also maintained offices in public hospitals and police stations. Women often were reluctant to file formal charges of abuse for social, cultural, and economic reasons.

The government could prosecute harassment via the penal code prohibition on "disgracing or dishonoring" a person in public, punishable by a minimum of one year in prison and as long as 15 years if the victim is younger than 14-years-old; an "infamous" act against the rules of decency, which carries a penalty of six months in prison; or "dishonoring a woman by word or deed on a public roadway," which could result in up to one year in prison and a 10,000 dirham (approximately $2,700) fine. However, such prosecutions rarely occurred in practice.

Couples and individuals had the right to decide freely and responsibly the number, spacing, and timing of their children, and to have the information and means to do so free from discrimination, coercion, and violence. According to the most recent UN estimates, the maternal mortality rate in the country was 10 deaths per 100,000 live births in 2008. A study released by the UAE Women's Federation in November noted that skilled medical personnel attended 99 percent of births. There was no information on prenatal and postnatal care. Statistics on the use of modern contraceptive methods accessible to both married and single women were unavailable; however, various contraceptives were widely available. There was no information on whether men and women are treated and diagnosed equally treatment for sexually transmitted infections, including HIV.

Women faced legal and economic discrimination. The government's interpretation of Sharia applied in personal status cases and family law. Muslim women were forbidden to marry non-Muslims. Unlike men, female citizens married to noncitizens did not automatically pass citizenship to their children. The law permits a man to have as many as four wives. Women normally inherited less than men under the government's interpretation of Sharia. For example, a son may inherit double what a daughter inherits when their parent dies.

In order for a woman to obtain a divorce with a financial settlement, she must prove that her husband has inflicted physical or moral harm upon her, has abandoned her for at least three months, or has not maintained her upkeep or that of their children. Alternatively women may divorce by paying compensation or surrendering their dowry to their husbands. The law gives divorced fathers custody of female children above the age of 13 and male children above the age of 10.

On August 23, the Federal Supreme Court ruled that, in decisions on child custody, the interests of the child come first. In the ruling, the court granted a divorced woman custody of her seven sons, despite the eldest being older than 10 years old. The court established a precedent essentially limiting the application of Sharia to custody cases.

Fornication outside of marriage is a crime, and the government may imprison and deport noncitizen women if they bear children out of wedlock. Paternity denial was an emerging problem in the courts. Despite DNA tests proving paternity, the courts could not force a man to accept paternal responsibility. In the absence of an acknowledged father, the mothers of these children faced potential legal charges of adultery, for which the punishment can be lashing, according to media reports.

No law prohibits women from working or owning businesses, and a man has no right under the government's interpretation of Sharia to ban his wife from working if she was employed at the time of their marriage; however, some husbands reportedly did so. Women who worked outside the home regularly did not receive equal benefits, and women also reportedly faced discrimination in promotions and earning equal wages.

Women constituted approximately 75 percent of university students. Coeducation is prohibited in public schools and universities except in the United Arab Emirate University's Executive MBA program. Several private schools, private universities, and institutions were coeducational.

Children

The government registered Bidoon births, but it did not grant citizenship to the children.

Education is compulsory through the ninth grade; however, compulsory education was not enforced, and some children did not attend school, especially children of noncitizens. Noncitizen children could enroll in public schools only if they scored at least 90 percent on entrance examinations, which were given only in Arabic. The government provided primary education free to citizens but not to noncitizens. Public schools were not coeducational after kindergarten. Statistically, girls and women in every age group were more academically successful and continued to higher levels of education than their male peers.

Child abuse was limited, and there was some evidence that societal influences prevented cases from being reported. The law protects children from abuse and trafficking, and the government provides some shelter and help for victims. The law does not address female genital mutilation (FGM), which some Somali, Omani, and Sudanese foreign residents practiced. The Ministry of Health prohibits hospitals and clinics from performing FGM.

The United Arab Emirates is not a party to the 1980 Hague Convention on the Civil Aspects of International Child Abduction. For information on international parental child abduction, please see the Department of State's annual report on

compliance at
http://travel.state.gov/abduction/resources/congressreport/congressreport_4308.html.

Anti-Semitism

There were no synagogues for the small foreign Jewish population in residence. Anti-Semitism was apparent in news articles and editorials. These expressions occurred primarily in daily newspapers without government response.

Trafficking in Persons

For information on trafficking in persons, please see the Department of State's annual *Trafficking in Persons Report* at www.state.gov/g/tip.

Persons with Disabilities

The law prohibits discrimination against persons who have physical and mental disabilities; however, such discrimination occurred in practice. Most public buildings provided some form of access for persons with disabilities in accordance with the law. Health care provided in the Ministry of Labor's five federal rehabilitation centers, as well as those in private centers, reportedly was inadequate.

Various departments within the ministries of labor and education were responsible for protecting the rights of persons with disabilities, and the government effectively enforced these rights. The government reserved 1 percent of all federal government jobs and 2 percent of government jobs in Abu Dhabi for persons with disabilities. On October 25, the Community Development Authority (CDA) in Dubai held a meeting with government and private sector human resource managers in an effort to promote employment opportunities for persons with disabilities. The CDA offers public and private corporations assistance in hiring persons with disabilities through a program called "Elkayt."

National/Racial/Ethnic Minorities

Approximately 80 percent of the country's residents were noncitizens originating primarily from the Indian subcontinent. Societal discrimination against noncitizens was prevalent and occurred in most areas of daily life, including employment, education, housing, social interaction, and health care.

In March the UN special rapporteur on contemporary forms of racism, racial discrimination, xenophobia, and related intolerance released a report on his October 2009 visit. The report noted the country's unique situation, where non-nationals represent the vast majority of the population, and that the influx of foreign workers created tremendous challenges for society. The report concluded that the country should enact legislation, improve policies, and implement them effectively.

Societal Abuses, Discrimination, and Acts of Violence Based on Sexual Orientation and Gender Identity

Both civil law and Sharia criminalize homosexual activity. Under Sharia the death penalty is the punishment for individuals who engage in consensual homosexual activity. There were no prosecutions for homosexual activity during the year. In 2009 there were reports that the government deported and sentenced individuals to prison for openly homosexual activity.

Under the law, cross-dressing is a punishable offense. The government deported cross-dressing foreign residents and referred citizens to public prosecutors. At times the government subjected persons to psychological treatment and counseling for homosexual activity.

Other Societal Violence or Discrimination

Persons with HIV/AIDS and other diseases faced discrimination. There were credible reports that government officials discriminated against prisoners with HIV by not granting commuted sentences or parole that other prisoners with similar records had received. Noncitizen residents infected with HIV, hepatitis types B and C, and tuberculosis were denied all health benefits, quarantined, and deported.

Section 7   Worker Rights

a.   The Right of Association

The law does not permit workers to form or join unions, and no unions existed. Professional organizations, such as lawyers' associations, existed; however, they had to receive government approval for international affiliations to exist and had to receive government approval for international affiliation.

The law does not prohibit strikes by private sector workers, but it allows an employer to suspend an employee for striking. In addition the government may cancel the work permit of and deport for up to one year any foreign worker who is absent from work for more than seven days without a valid reason.

The government forbids strikes by public sector employees, citing national security. A public sector employee may file an administrative grievance or a case in the civil courts to address a labor-related dispute or complaint; however, there was no evidence of any such grievances or cases.

The government generally did not punish workers for nonviolent protests in response to nonpayment of wages by employers, but it dispersed such protests during the year. Most grievances were related to unpaid wages and hazardous or abusive working conditions. The Ministry of Labor generally contacted the business owner, which usually prompted a settlement privately.

b. The Right to Organize and Bargain Collectively

Employees covered by the labor law--which excludes domestic, agricultural, and government workers--may file collective employment dispute complaints with the Ministry of Labor in person or via telephone, which serves as mediator between the parties. Employees may file unresolved disputes with the labor court system, which are in turn forwarded to the conciliation council. In practice most cases were resolved through direct negotiation. The government granted some professional associations with a majority citizen membership a limited ability to raise work-related issues, to petition the government for redress, and to file grievances with the government. Foreign workers may belong to these professional associations as well; however, they do not have voting rights and cannot serve on the organizations' boards.

Businesses in free trade zones (FTZs) are not subject to labor statutes. The Ministry of Labor does not regulate the FTZs; instead, each FTZ maintained its own labor department. Unions and strikes are not allowed in any FTZs.

c. Prohibition of Forced or Compulsory Labor

The law prohibits forced or compulsory labor, including by children; however, such practices occurred, predominantly involving migrant workers from South and East Asia who work as construction workers or as domestic employees.

Many migrant workers were subjected to forced labor conditions such as restrictions on movement and communication, nonpayment of wages, and physical and sexual abuse. Reports of worker suicides continued. There were reports that some female migrant workers were forced into prostitution. Upon arrival to the country, some foreign workers signed contracts that had lower salaries or involved a different type of work than what was stated in contracts signed in their country of origin. This practice was known as "contract switching."

Foreign workers frequently did not receive their wages, sometimes for extended periods. In 2008, to reduce the problem of unpaid wages, the Ministry of Labor and the Central Bank signed a memorandum of understanding that facilitated direct deposits of laborers' salaries, creating the Wage Protection System. On August 26, the government announced that 500,000 laborers were receiving their wages in this manner and set a May 31 deadline for all employers to adopt the system, which would cover more than four million workers. In contrast to 2009 when 500,000 workers received their salaries electronically, during the year 1.8 million workers enrolled in the Wage Protection System, according to the Ministry of Labor, which the government claimed represents 100 percent of workers.

Some domestic and agricultural workers were subjected to unpaid labor to repay their employers for hiring expenses. In most cases, the workers paid recruitment fees to the recruiter in their country of origin and were responsible for repaying them once beginning work. Employers routinely held employees' passports, severely restricting their freedom of movement. There were increasing incidents of employees prevented from changing jobs because their contracts stipulated that they were prohibited from working for a "competitor" for six months after their original employment ended. The only way to overcome the six-month restriction was to seek a letter of "no objection" from the original employer; some employers, as retribution for losing the employee to another employer, refused to sign such letters. Employees lack any recourse if this happens; they must leave the country and reenter. In December authorities announced a change in labor laws, effective in 2011, removing the requirement for employees to obtain a no objection certificate.

The Ministry of Labor made exceptions during the year by not requiring "no objection" letters if the employee had completed three years in the original position or if the employer had withheld salary.

In May local media reported that more than 1,000 workers in a labor camp outside Sharjah were stranded without work, wages, or legal residency documentation after their employer went bankrupt. On August 31, 700 foreign workers outside Sharjah, abandoned by their employer, were without access to food or water. In both cases, local charities provided food for the workers, who were seeking redress from the courts. The Ministry of Labor worked to repatriate the individuals eventually.

In another case in Ajman, workers were abandoned by their employer. Since these individuals were under contract to the Ministry of Education, the Ministry of Labor worked to repatriate the workers or find them new employers in the country.

Also see the Department of State's annual *Trafficking in Persons Report* at www.state.gov/g/tip.

d.   Prohibition of Child Labor and Minimum Age for Employment

The law prohibits employment of persons younger than the age of 15 and has special provisions for employing persons between 15 and 18 years of age, including foreign resident children 16-years-old or older. The Ministry of Labor is responsible for enforcing these regulations and generally enforced them effectively. However, there were reports of foreign children who came to the country under their parents' work permits and subsequently were pressured to work. Additionally the traditional practice of using children as camel jockeys resumed in some privately held races.

Also see the Department of State's annual *Trafficking in Persons Report* at www.state.gov/g/tip.

e.   Acceptable Conditions of Work

There is no established minimum wage, leaving much of the workforce without sufficient compensation for more than minimal subsistence. The average daily wage did provide a decent standard of living for a worker and family. Salaries, which depend on the occupation and employer, were estimated to be at least 400 dirhams (approximately $110) per month for domestic or agricultural workers and 600 dirhams (approximately $164) per month for construction workers. Highly skilled and white-collar employees generally received much higher salaries.

According to the labor law, the workday is eight hours and the workweek six days; however, these standards were not monitored or enforced. There were laws regulating minimum rest periods and hours worked, which varied depending on the nature of the work. There was no legal provision requiring overtime pay, nor was there a prohibition on excessive compulsory overtime. Domestic workers are under the jurisdiction of the Ministry of Interior, which has a special office for assisting domestic laborers; labor laws do not apply to domestic workers. The unregulated conditions of domestic workers left them vulnerable to long hours and underpayment.

The Ministry of Labor extended the required summer midday work break from two months to three months for most outdoor laborers. This requirement begins in June and lasts until September. However, during July and August, the hottest months of the year, the government exempted oil, asphalt, and cement companies from following the law. The government routinely fined employers for violating the midday break rule and published compliance statistics. For the first offense, an employer is fined 10,000 dirhams (approximately $2,725) and is prohibited from issuing obtaining new labor permits for three months. A second offense results in a 20,000 dirham fine (approximately $5,450) and a six-month prohibition. A third offense carries a 30,000 dirham fine (approximately $8,175) and a one-year prohibition on new permits.

The Ministry of Labor operated a toll-free hotline through which workers were able to report companies that violated break rules or delayed wage payments.

The law requires employers to provide employees with a safe work and living environment; however, despite recent increases in the number of labor inspectors, the government did not uniformly enforce health and safety standards. The ministry hired additional safety and health inspectors, bringing the total to more than 450. Inspections of workplaces--primarily construction sites--took place throughout the year, resulting in fines for employers who violated workplace safety or midday break rules. The ministry also employed language interpreters to assist foreign workers in understanding employment guidelines.

Despite efforts to improve housing facilities, some low-skilled and foreign employees continued to face substandard living conditions, including overcrowded apartments or lodging in unsafe and unhygienic "labor camps," which sometimes lacked electricity, potable water, and adequate cooking and bathing facilities. Construction of newer worker accommodations was ongoing. Individual emirates enforced their own standards for minimum conditions for labor accommodations.

During the year the press reported a number of cases where workers were injured or killed on job sites due to inadequate safety measures. Although the law requires the government to monitor job-related injuries and deaths, in practice the government registered the cases but did not consistently follow up on them.

Domestic workers routinely were subject to physical, sexual, and emotional abuse. There were reports that employers withheld the passports of their domestic workers; in some cases, they prevented workers from leaving the country. In August 2009 police in Ajman arrested a woman accused of beating her maid with an electrical cord, breaking her ribs, and burning her feet with an iron. Updated information on the court case was unavailable during the year.

Workers' jobs were not protected if they removed themselves from what they considered to be unsafe working conditions; however, all workers have the right to lodge labor-related grievances to the Ministry of Labor. If ministry arbitration could not resolve the issue, it was referred to the judiciary.